MY PET
BEARDED DRAGONS
LOGBOOK

THIS BOOK BELONGS TO:

....

....

ALL ABOUT YOUR DRAGONS

PHOTO/DRAWING

 NICKNAME:

CHARACTERTICS:

 HABITAT:

 COLOR/MARKING:

NOTES:

OWNER'S INFORMATION

NAME:

ADDRESS:

PHONE: EMAIL:

DRAGONS'S INFORMATION

NAME: DATE OF BIRTH:

GENDER: ADOPTION PLACE:

PHONE: SPECIES:

BREED: MICROCHIP:

LICENSE#:

COLOR & MARKING:

VET INFORMATION

CLINIC: VET:

ADDRESS:

PHONE: EMAIL:

GROWTH CHART

DATE	AGE	WEIGHT	LENGHT	NOTES

GROWTH CHART

DATE	AGE	WEIGHT	LENGHT	NOTES

DRAGONS MEDICATION

MEDICATION	DATE:	NOTES:

ABOUT BEARDED DRAGONS

Diet

- Leafy vegetables and insects

Life
Expectancy:

- 7-12 years

Length, Weight:

- 15 to 20 inches,
- 230 to 520 grams

UVB and
infrared lights

- 30%-40% humidity,
- 95°F-105°F basking area,
- 80°F during the day

ROUTINE CARE, DIET

DAILY ACTIVITY

 Feed your dragons

 Change your dragon's water daily.

 Dusting powder on food 1 x / 2-3 day.

 Spot clean soiled areas.

 Remove any uneaten live food

 Check temperatures / humidity

 Visually inspect Bearded Dragon

WEEKLY ACTIVITY

 Clean glass.

 Top up substrate.

 Clean any decorative rocks, plants etc.

 Physically inspect your dragon.

 Bathing dragon & trim toenails.

 Weigh & record data

BEARDED DRAGON CHECKLIST

 Daily Activity

WEEK OF [ ] DATE [ ]

	SUN	MON	TUE	WED	THU	FRI	SAT
Feed your dragons daily.	○	○	○	○	○	○	○
Change water daily.	○	○	○	○	○	○	○
Dusting powder on food 1 x / 2-3 day.	○	○	○	○	○	○	○
Remove any uneaten live food	○	○	○	○	○	○	○
Spot clean soiled areas	○	○	○	○	○	○	○
Check temperatures / humidity	○	○	○	○	○	○	○
Visually inspect Bearded Dragon	○	○	○	○	○	○	○

NOTES:

BEARDED DRAGON CHECKLIST

📅 DATE: _____   📅 DATE: _____

WEEKLY ACTIVITY

○ Clean glass

○ Top up substrate

○ Clean any decorative rocks, plants etc

○ Physically inspect your dragon

○ Bathing dragon &
trim toenails once a week

○ Weigh & record data

HEALTH CHECKLIST

○ Active and alert

○ Clear eyes

○ Body and tail are
filled out

○ Healthy skin

○ Clear nose and vent

○ Eats regularly

DIARY / NOTES:

BEARDED DRAGON CHECKLIST

 Daily Activity

WEEK OF [ ] DATE [   ]

Activity	SUN	MON	TUE	WED	THU	FRI	SAT
Feed your dragons daily.	○	○	○	○	○	○	○
Change water daily.	○	○	○	○	○	○	○
Dusting powder on food 1 x / 2-3 day.	○	○	○	○	○	○	○
Remove any uneaten live food	○	○	○	○	○	○	○
Spot clean soiled areas	○	○	○	○	○	○	○
Check temperatures / humidity	○	○	○	○	○	○	○
Visually inspect Bearded Dragon	○	○	○	○	○	○	○

NOTES:

BEARDED DRAGON CHECKLIST

📅 DATE: _____   📅 DATE: _____

WEEKLY ACTIVITY

- ○ Clean glass
- ○ Top up substrate
- ○ Clean any decorative rocks, plants etc
- ○ Physically inspect your dragon
- ○ Bathing dragon & trim toenails once a week
- ○ Weigh & record data

HEALTH CHECKLIST

- ○ Active and alert
- ○ Clear eyes
- ○ Body and tail are filled out
- ○ Healthy skin
- ○ Clear nose and vent
- ○ Eats regularly

DIARY / NOTES:

BEARDED DRAGON CHECKLIST

 Daily Activity

WEEK OF [   ] DATE [   ]

	SUN	MON	TUE	WED	THU	FRI	SAT
Feed your dragons daily.	○	○	○	○	○	○	○
Change water daily.	○	○	○	○	○	○	○
Dusting powder on food 1 x / 2-3 day.	○	○	○	○	○	○	○
Remove any uneaten live food	○	○	○	○	○	○	○
Spot clean soiled areas	○	○	○	○	○	○	○
Check temperatures / humidity	○	○	○	○	○	○	○
Visually inspect Bearded Dragon	○	○	○	○	○	○	○

NOTES:

BEARDED DRAGON CHECKLIST

📅 DATE: _____

📅 DATE: _____

WEEKLY ACTIVITY

○ Clean glass

○ Top up substrate

○ Clean any decorative rocks, plants etc

○ Physically inspect your dragon

○ Bathing dragon & trim toenails once a week

○ Weigh & record data

HEALTH CHECKLIST

○ Active and alert

○ Clear eyes

○ Body and tail are filled out

○ Healthy skin

○ Clear nose and vent

○ Eats regularly

DIARY / NOTES:

BEARDED DRAGON CHECKLIST

	Daily Activity	SUN	MON	TUE	WED	THU	FRI	SAT
	WEEK OF ____ DATE ____							
	Feed your dragons daily.	○	○	○	○	○	○	○
	Change water daily.	○	○	○	○	○	○	○
	Dusting powder on food 1 x / 2-3 day.	○	○	○	○	○	○	○
	Remove any uneaten live food	○	○	○	○	○	○	○
	Spot clean soiled areas	○	○	○	○	○	○	○
	Check temperatures / humidity	○	○	○	○	○	○	○
	Visually inspect Bearded Dragon	○	○	○	○	○	○	○

NOTES:

BEARDED DRAGON CHECKLIST

📅 DATE: _____   📅 DATE: _____

WEEKLY ACTIVITY

- ⚪ Clean glass
- ⚪ Top up substrate
- ⚪ Clean any decorative rocks, plants etc
- ⚪ Physically inspect your dragon
- ⚪ Bathing dragon & trim toenails once a week
- ⚪ Weigh & record data

HEALTH CHECKLIST

- ⚪ Active and alert
- ⚪ Clear eyes
- ⚪ Body and tail are filled out
- ⚪ Healthy skin
- ⚪ Clear nose and vent
- ⚪ Eats regularly

DIARY / NOTES:

BEARDED DRAGON CHECKLIST

 Daily Activity

WEEK OF ☐ DATE ☐

	SUN	MON	TUE	WED	THU	FRI	SAT
Feed your dragons daily.	○	○	○	○	○	○	○
Change water daily.	○	○	○	○	○	○	○
Dusting powder on food 1 x / 2-3 day.	○	○	○	○	○	○	○
Remove any uneaten live food	○	○	○	○	○	○	○
Spot clean soiled areas	○	○	○	○	○	○	○
Check temperatures / humidity	○	○	○	○	○	○	○
Visually inspect Bearded Dragon	○	○	○	○	○	○	○

NOTES:

BEARDED DRAGON CHECKLIST

📅 DATE: _____   📅 DATE: _____

WEEKLY ACTIVITY   ## HEALTH CHECKLIST

○ Clean glass   ○ Active and alert

○ Top up substrate   ○ Clear eyes

○ Clean any decorative rocks, plants etc   ○ Body and tail are filled out

○ Physically inspect your dragon ○ Healthy skin

○ Bathing dragon & trim toenails once a week   ○ Clear nose and vent

○ Weigh & record data   ○ Eats regularly

DIARY / NOTES:

BEARDED DRAGON CHECKLIST

 Daily Activity

WEEK OF [ ] DATE [ ]

	SUN	MON	TUE	WED	THU	FRI	SAT
Feed your dragons daily.	○	○	○	○	○	○	○
Change water daily.	○	○	○	○	○	○	○
Dusting powder on food 1 x / 2-3 day.	○	○	○	○	○	○	○
Remove any uneaten live food	○	○	○	○	○	○	○
Spot clean soiled areas	○	○	○	○	○	○	○
Check temperatures / humidity	○	○	○	○	○	○	○
Visually inspect Bearded Dragon	○	○	○	○	○	○	○

NOTES:

BEARDED DRAGON CHECKLIST

📅 DATE: [_____]

📅 DATE: [_____]

WEEKLY ACTIVITY

- ○ Clean glass
- ○ Top up substrate
- ○ Clean any decorative rocks, plants etc
- ○ Physically inspect your dragon
- ○ Bathing dragon & trim toenails once a week
- ○ Weigh & record data

HEALTH CHECKLIST

- ○ Active and alert
- ○ Clear eyes
- ○ Body and tail are filled out
- ○ Healthy skin
- ○ Clear nose and vent
- ○ Eats regularly

DIARY / NOTES:

BEARDED DRAGON CHECKLIST

 Daily Activity

WEEK OF [   ] DATE [   ]

Activity	SUN	MON	TUE	WED	THU	FRI	SAT
Feed your dragons daily.	○	○	○	○	○	○	○
Change water daily.	○	○	○	○	○	○	○
Dusting powder on food 1 x / 2-3 day.	○	○	○	○	○	○	○
Remove any uneaten live food	○	○	○	○	○	○	○
Spot clean soiled areas	○	○	○	○	○	○	○
Check temperatures / humidity	○	○	○	○	○	○	○
Visually inspect Bearded Dragon	○	○	○	○	○	○	○

NOTES:

BEARDED DRAGON CHECKLIST

📅 DATE: _____   📅 DATE: _____

WEEKLY ACTIVITY

○ Clean glass

○ Top up substrate

○ Clean any decorative rocks, plants etc

○ Physically inspect your dragon

○ Bathing dragon &
  trim toenails once a week

○ Weigh & record data

HEALTH CHECKLIST

○ Active and alert

○ Clear eyes

○ Body and tail are
  filled out

○ Healthy skin

○ Clear nose and vent

○ Eats regularly

DIARY / NOTES:

BEARDED DRAGON CHECKLIST

Daily Activity	WEEK OF _____ DATE _____						
	SUN	MON	TUE	WED	THU	FRI	SAT
Feed your dragons daily.	○	○	○	○	○	○	○
Change water daily.	○	○	○	○	○	○	○
Dusting powder on food 1 x / 2-3 day.	○	○	○	○	○	○	○
Remove any uneaten live food	○	○	○	○	○	○	○
Spot clean soiled areas	○	○	○	○	○	○	○
Check temperatures / humidity	○	○	○	○	○	○	○
Visually inspect Bearded Dragon	○	○	○	○	○	○	○

NOTES:

BEARDED DRAGON CHECKLIST

📅 DATE: _____   📅 DATE: _____

WEEKLY ACTIVITY

- ○ Clean glass
- ○ Top up substrate
- ○ Clean any decorative rocks, plants etc
- ○ Physically inspect your dragon
- ○ Bathing dragon & trim toenails once a week
- ○ Weigh & record data

HEALTH CHECKLIST

- ○ Active and alert
- ○ Clear eyes
- ○ Body and tail are filled out
- ○ Healthy skin
- ○ Clear nose and vent
- ○ Eats regularly

DIARY / NOTES:

BEARDED DRAGON CHECKLIST

 Daily Activity

WEEK OF [   ] DATE [   ]

	SUN	MON	TUE	WED	THU	FRI	SAT
Feed your dragons daily.	○	○	○	○	○	○	○
Change water daily.	○	○	○	○	○	○	○
Dusting powder on food 1 x / 2-3 day.	○	○	○	○	○	○	○
Remove any uneaten live food	○	○	○	○	○	○	○
Spot clean soiled areas	○	○	○	○	○	○	○
Check temperatures / humidity	○	○	○	○	○	○	○
Visually inspect Bearded Dragon	○	○	○	○	○	○	○

NOTES:

BEARDED DRAGON CHECKLIST

📅 DATE: _____   📅 DATE: _____

WEEKLY ACTIVITY

○ Clean glass

○ Top up substrate

○ Clean any decorative rocks, plants etc

○ Physically inspect your dragon

○ Bathing dragon &
trim toenails once a week

○ Weigh & record data

HEALTH CHECKLIST

○ Active and alert

○ Clear eyes

○ Body and tail are
filled out

○ Healthy skin

○ Clear nose and vent

○ Eats regularly

DIARY / NOTES:

BEARDED DRAGON CHECKLIST

 Daily Activity

WEEK OF [   ] DATE [   ]

	SUN	MON	TUE	WED	THU	FRI	SAT
Feed your dragons daily.	○	○	○	○	○	○	○
Change water daily.	○	○	○	○	○	○	○
Dusting powder on food 1 x / 2-3 day.	○	○	○	○	○	○	○
Remove any uneaten live food	○	○	○	○	○	○	○
Spot clean soiled areas	○	○	○	○	○	○	○
Check temperatures / humidity	○	○	○	○	○	○	○
Visually inspect Bearded Dragon	○	○	○	○	○	○	○

NOTES:

BEARDED DRAGON CHECKLIST

📅 DATE: _____   📅 DATE: _____

WEEKLY ACTIVITY

○ Clean glass

○ Top up substrate

○ Clean any decorative rocks, plants etc

○ Physically inspect your dragon

○ Bathing dragon &
trim toenails once a week

○ Weigh & record data

HEALTH CHECKLIST

○ Active and alert

○ Clear eyes

○ Body and tail are
filled out

○ Healthy skin

○ Clear nose and vent

○ Eats regularly

DIARY / NOTES:

BEARDED DRAGON CHECKLIST

 Daily Activity

WEEK OF _____ DATE _____

Activity	SUN	MON	TUE	WED	THU	FRI	SAT
Feed your dragons daily.	○	○	○	○	○	○	○
Change water daily.	○	○	○	○	○	○	○
Dusting powder on food 1 x / 2-3 day.	○	○	○	○	○	○	○
Remove any uneaten live food	○	○	○	○	○	○	○
Spot clean soiled areas	○	○	○	○	○	○	○
Check temperatures / humidity	○	○	○	○	○	○	○
Visually inspect Bearded Dragon	○	○	○	○	○	○	○

NOTES:

BEARDED DRAGON CHECKLIST

📅 DATE: _____   📅 DATE: _____

WEEKLY ACTIVITY

○ Clean glass

○ Top up substrate

○ Clean any decorative rocks, plants etc

○ Physically inspect your dragon

○ Bathing dragon &
trim toenails once a week

○ Weigh & record data

HEALTH CHECKLIST

○ Active and alert

○ Clear eyes

○ Body and tail are
filled out

○ Healthy skin

○ Clear nose and vent

○ Eats regularly

DIARY / NOTES:

BEARDED DRAGON CHECKLIST

 Daily Activity

WEEK OF ☐ DATE ☐

	SUN	MON	TUE	WED	THU	FRI	SAT
Feed your dragons daily.	○	○	○	○	○	○	○
Change water daily.	○	○	○	○	○	○	○
Dusting powder on food 1 x / 2-3 day.	○	○	○	○	○	○	○
Remove any uneaten live food	○	○	○	○	○	○	○
Spot clean soiled areas	○	○	○	○	○	○	○
Check temperatures / humidity	○	○	○	○	○	○	○
Visually inspect Bearded Dragon	○	○	○	○	○	○	○

NOTES:

BEARDED DRAGON CHECKLIST

📅 DATE: _____

📅 DATE: _____

WEEKLY ACTIVITY

- ○ Clean glass
- ○ Top up substrate
- ○ Clean any decorative rocks, plants etc
- ○ Physically inspect your dragon
- ○ Bathing dragon & trim toenails once a week
- ○ Weigh & record data

HEALTH CHECKLIST

- ○ Active and alert
- ○ Clear eyes
- ○ Body and tail are filled out
- ○ Healthy skin
- ○ Clear nose and vent
- ○ Eats regularly

DIARY / NOTES:

BEARDED DRAGON CHECKLIST

Daily Activity	WEEK OF _____ DATE _____						
	SUN	MON	TUE	WED	THU	FRI	SAT
Feed your dragons daily.	○	○	○	○	○	○	○
Change water daily.	○	○	○	○	○	○	○
Dusting powder on food 1 x / 2-3 day.	○	○	○	○	○	○	○
Remove any uneaten live food	○	○	○	○	○	○	○
Spot clean soiled areas	○	○	○	○	○	○	○
Check temperatures / humidity	○	○	○	○	○	○	○
Visually inspect Bearded Dragon	○	○	○	○	○	○	○

NOTES:

BEARDED DRAGON CHECKLIST

📅 DATE: _____   📅 DATE: _____

WEEKLY ACTIVITY

○ Clean glass

○ Top up substrate

○ Clean any decorative rocks, plants etc

○ Physically inspect your dragon

○ Bathing dragon &
trim toenails once a week

○ Weigh & record data

HEALTH CHECKLIST

○ Active and alert

○ Clear eyes

○ Body and tail are
filled out

○ Healthy skin

○ Clear nose and vent

○ Eats regularly

DIARY / NOTES:

BEARDED DRAGON CHECKLIST

Daily Activity	WEEK OF [ ] DATE [ ]						
	SUN	MON	TUE	WED	THU	FRI	SAT
Feed your dragons daily.	○	○	○	○	○	○	○
Change water daily.	○	○	○	○	○	○	○
Dusting powder on food 1 x / 2-3 day.	○	○	○	○	○	○	○
Remove any uneaten live food	○	○	○	○	○	○	○
Spot clean soiled areas	○	○	○	○	○	○	○
Check temperatures / humidity	○	○	○	○	○	○	○
Visually inspect Bearded Dragon	○	○	○	○	○	○	○

NOTES:

BEARDED DRAGON CHECKLIST

📅 DATE: _____   📅 DATE: _____

WEEKLY ACTIVITY

- ○ Clean glass
- ○ Top up substrate
- ○ Clean any decorative rocks, plants etc
- ○ Physically inspect your dragon
- ○ Bathing dragon & trim toenails once a week
- ○ Weigh & record data

HEALTH CHECKLIST

- ○ Active and alert
- ○ Clear eyes
- ○ Body and tail are filled out
- ○ Healthy skin
- ○ Clear nose and vent
- ○ Eats regularly

DIARY / NOTES:

BEARDED DRAGON CHECKLIST

 Daily Activity

WEEK OF ___ DATE ___

	SUN	MON	TUE	WED	THU	FRI	SAT
Feed your dragons daily.	◯	◯	◯	◯	◯	◯	◯
Change water daily.	◯	◯	◯	◯	◯	◯	◯
Dusting powder on food 1 x / 2-3 day.	◯	◯	◯	◯	◯	◯	◯
Remove any uneaten live food	◯	◯	◯	◯	◯	◯	◯
Spot clean soiled areas	◯	◯	◯	◯	◯	◯	◯
Check temperatures / humidity	◯	◯	◯	◯	◯	◯	◯
Visually inspect Bearded Dragon	◯	◯	◯	◯	◯	◯	◯

NOTES:

BEARDED DRAGON CHECKLIST

📅 DATE:

📅 DATE:

WEEKLY ACTIVITY

Clean glass

Top up substrate

Clean any decorative rocks, plants etc

Physically inspect your dragon

Bathing dragon &
trim toenails once a week

Weigh & record data

HEALTH CHECKLIST

Active and alert

Clear eyes

Body and tail are
filled out

Healthy skin

Clear nose and vent

Eats regularly

DIARY / NOTES:

BEARDED DRAGON CHECKLIST

Daily Activity	WEEK OF [ ] DATE [ ]						
	SUN	MON	TUE	WED	THU	FRI	SAT
Feed your dragons daily.	○	○	○	○	○	○	○
Change water daily.	○	○	○	○	○	○	○
Dusting powder on food 1 x / 2-3 day.	○	○	○	○	○	○	○
Remove any uneaten live food	○	○	○	○	○	○	○
Spot clean soiled areas	○	○	○	○	○	○	○
Check temperatures / humidity	○	○	○	○	○	○	○
Visually inspect Bearded Dragon	○	○	○	○	○	○	○

NOTES:

BEARDED DRAGON CHECKLIST

📅 DATE: _____

📅 DATE: _____

WEEKLY ACTIVITY

- ○ Clean glass
- ○ Top up substrate
- ○ Clean any decorative rocks, plants etc
- ○ Physically inspect your dragon
- ○ Bathing dragon & trim toenails once a week
- ○ Weigh & record data

HEALTH CHECKLIST

- ○ Active and alert
- ○ Clear eyes
- ○ Body and tail are filled out
- ○ Healthy skin
- ○ Clear nose and vent
- ○ Eats regularly

DIARY / NOTES:

BEARDED DRAGON CHECKLIST

 Daily Activity

	WEEK OF _____ DATE _____							
		SUN	MON	TUE	WED	THU	FRI	SAT

	Activity	SUN	MON	TUE	WED	THU	FRI	SAT
	Feed your dragons daily.	○	○	○	○	○	○	○
	Change water daily.	○	○	○	○	○	○	○
	Dusting powder on food 1 x / 2-3 day.	○	○	○	○	○	○	○
	Remove any uneaten live food	○	○	○	○	○	○	○
	Spot clean soiled areas	○	○	○	○	○	○	○
	Check temperatures / humidity	○	○	○	○	○	○	○
	Visually inspect Bearded Dragon	○	○	○	○	○	○	○

NOTES:

BEARDED DRAGON CHECKLIST

📅 DATE: _____

📅 DATE: _____

WEEKLY ACTIVITY

○ Clean glass

○ Top up substrate

○ Clean any decorative rocks, plants etc

○ Physically inspect your dragon

○ Bathing dragon &
trim toenails once a week

○ Weigh & record data

HEALTH CHECKLIST

○ Active and alert

○ Clear eyes

○ Body and tail are
filled out

○ Healthy skin

○ Clear nose and vent

○ Eats regularly

DIARY / NOTES:

BEARDED DRAGON CHECKLIST

 Daily Activity

	WEEK OF	DATE						
	SUN	MON	TUE	WED	THU	FRI	SAT	

Activity	SUN	MON	TUE	WED	THU	FRI	SAT
Feed your dragons daily.	○	○	○	○	○	○	○
Change water daily.	○	○	○	○	○	○	○
Dusting powder on food 1 x / 2-3 day.	○	○	○	○	○	○	○
Remove any uneaten live food	○	○	○	○	○	○	○
Spot clean soiled areas	○	○	○	○	○	○	○
Check temperatures / humidity	○	○	○	○	○	○	○
Visually inspect Bearded Dragon	○	○	○	○	○	○	○

NOTES:

BEARDED DRAGON CHECKLIST

📅 DATE: _____   📅 DATE: _____

WEEKLY ACTIVITY

- ◯ Clean glass
- ◯ Top up substrate
- ◯ Clean any decorative rocks, plants etc
- ◯ Physically inspect your dragon
- ◯ Bathing dragon & trim toenails once a week
- ◯ Weigh & record data

HEALTH CHECKLIST

- ◯ Active and alert
- ◯ Clear eyes
- ◯ Body and tail are filled out
- ◯ Healthy skin
- ◯ Clear nose and vent
- ◯ Eats regularly

DIARY / NOTES:

BEARDED DRAGON CHECKLIST

	Daily Activity	WEEK OF	DATE						
		SUN	MON	TUE	WED	THU	FRI	SAT
	Feed your dragons daily.	○	○	○	○	○	○	○
	Change water daily.	○	○	○	○	○	○	○
	Dusting powder on food 1 x / 2-3 day.	○	○	○	○	○	○	○
	Remove any uneaten live food	○	○	○	○	○	○	○
	Spot clean soiled areas	○	○	○	○	○	○	○
	Check temperatures / humidity	○	○	○	○	○	○	○
	Visually inspect Bearded Dragon	○	○	○	○	○	○	○

NOTES:

BEARDED DRAGON CHECKLIST

📅 DATE: ⬜

📅 DATE: ⬜

WEEKLY ACTIVITY

○ Clean glass

○ Top up substrate

○ Clean any decorative rocks, plants etc

○ Physically inspect your dragon

○ Bathing dragon &
trim toenails once a week

○ Weigh & record data

HEALTH CHECKLIST

○ Active and alert

○ Clear eyes

○ Body and tail are
filled out

○ Healthy skin

○ Clear nose and vent

○ Eats regularly

DIARY / NOTES:

BEARDED DRAGON CHECKLIST

 Daily Activity

	WEEK OF	DATE					
	SUN	MON	TUE	WED	THU	FRI	SAT
Feed your dragons daily.	○	○	○	○	○	○	○
Change water daily.	○	○	○	○	○	○	○
Dusting powder on food 1 x / 2-3 day.	○	○	○	○	○	○	○
Remove any uneaten live food	○	○	○	○	○	○	○
Spot clean soiled areas	○	○	○	○	○	○	○
Check temperatures / humidity	○	○	○	○	○	○	○
Visually inspect Bearded Dragon	○	○	○	○	○	○	○

NOTES:

BEARDED DRAGON CHECKLIST

📅 DATE: _____   📅 DATE: _____

WEEKLY ACTIVITY

- ○ Clean glass
- ○ Top up substrate
- ○ Clean any decorative rocks, plants etc
- ○ Physically inspect your dragon
- ○ Bathing dragon & trim toenails once a week
- ○ Weigh & record data

HEALTH CHECKLIST

- ○ Active and alert
- ○ Clear eyes
- ○ Body and tail are filled out
- ○ Healthy skin
- ○ Clear nose and vent
- ○ Eats regularly

DIARY / NOTES:

BEARDED DRAGON CHECKLIST

 Daily Activity

WEEK OF ___ DATE ___

	SUN	MON	TUE	WED	THU	FRI	SAT
Feed your dragons daily.	○	○	○	○	○	○	○
Change water daily.	○	○	○	○	○	○	○
Dusting powder on food 1 x / 2-3 day.	○	○	○	○	○	○	○
Remove any uneaten live food	○	○	○	○	○	○	○
Spot clean soiled areas	○	○	○	○	○	○	○
Check temperatures / humidity	○	○	○	○	○	○	○
Visually inspect Bearded Dragon	○	○	○	○	○	○	○

NOTES:

BEARDED DRAGON CHECKLIST

📅 DATE:

📅 DATE:

WEEKLY ACTIVITY

Clean glass

Top up substrate

Clean any decorative rocks, plants etc

Physically inspect your dragon

Bathing dragon &
trim toenails once a week

Weigh & record data

HEALTH CHECKLIST

Active and alert

Clear eyes

Body and tail are
filled out

Healthy skin

Clear nose and vent

Eats regularly

DIARY / NOTES:

BEARDED DRAGON CHECKLIST

Daily Activity	WEEK OF [ ] DATE [ ]						
	SUN	MON	TUE	WED	THU	FRI	SAT
Feed your dragons daily.	○	○	○	○	○	○	○
Change water daily.	○	○	○	○	○	○	○
Dusting powder on food 1 x / 2-3 day.	○	○	○	○	○	○	○
Remove any uneaten live food	○	○	○	○	○	○	○
Spot clean soiled areas	○	○	○	○	○	○	○
Check temperatures / humidity	○	○	○	○	○	○	○
Visually inspect Bearded Dragon	○	○	○	○	○	○	○

NOTES:

BEARDED DRAGON CHECKLIST

📅 DATE: _____   📅 DATE: _____

WEEKLY ACTIVITY

- ○ Clean glass
- ○ Top up substrate
- ○ Clean any decorative rocks, plants etc
- ○ Physically inspect your dragon
- ○ Bathing dragon & trim toenails once a week
- ○ Weigh & record data

HEALTH CHECKLIST

- ○ Active and alert
- ○ Clear eyes
- ○ Body and tail are filled out
- ○ Healthy skin
- ○ Clear nose and vent
- ○ Eats regularly

DIARY / NOTES:

BEARDED DRAGON CHECKLIST

Daily Activity	WEEK OF _____ DATE _____						
	SUN	MON	TUE	WED	THU	FRI	SAT
Feed your dragons daily.	◯	◯	◯	◯	◯	◯	◯
Change water daily.	◯	◯	◯	◯	◯	◯	◯
Dusting powder on food 1 x / 2-3 day.	◯	◯	◯	◯	◯	◯	◯
Remove any uneaten live food	◯	◯	◯	◯	◯	◯	◯
Spot clean soiled areas	◯	◯	◯	◯	◯	◯	◯
Check temperatures / humidity	◯	◯	◯	◯	◯	◯	◯
Visually inspect Bearded Dragon	◯	◯	◯	◯	◯	◯	◯

NOTES:

BEARDED DRAGON CHECKLIST

📅 DATE: 📅 DATE:

WEEKLY ACTIVITY

Clean glass

Top up substrate

Clean any decorative rocks, plants etc

Physically inspect your dragon

Bathing dragon &
trim toenails once a week

Weigh & record data

HEALTH CHECKLIST

Active and alert

Clear eyes

Body and tail are
filled out

Healthy skin

Clear nose and vent

Eats regularly

DIARY / NOTES:

BEARDED DRAGON CHECKLIST

Daily Activity	WEEK OF ____ DATE _____						
	SUN	MON	TUE	WED	THU	FRI	SAT
Feed your dragons daily.	○	○	○	○	○	○	○
Change water daily.	○	○	○	○	○	○	○
Dusting powder on food 1 x / 2-3 day.	○	○	○	○	○	○	○
Remove any uneaten live food	○	○	○	○	○	○	○
Spot clean soiled areas	○	○	○	○	○	○	○
Check temperatures / humidity	○	○	○	○	○	○	○
Visually inspect Bearded Dragon	○	○	○	○	○	○	○

NOTES:

BEARDED DRAGON CHECKLIST

📅 DATE: _____   📅 DATE: _____

WEEKLY ACTIVITY

- ⚪ Clean glass
- ⚪ Top up substrate
- ⚪ Clean any decorative rocks, plants etc
- ⚪ Physically inspect your dragon
- ⚪ Bathing dragon & trim toenails once a week
- ⚪ Weigh & record data

HEALTH CHECKLIST

- ⚪ Active and alert
- ⚪ Clear eyes
- ⚪ Body and tail are filled out
- ⚪ Healthy skin
- ⚪ Clear nose and vent
- ⚪ Eats regularly

DIARY / NOTES:

BEARDED DRAGON CHECKLIST

 Daily Activity

WEEK OF [   ] DATE [   ]

	SUN	MON	TUE	WED	THU	FRI	SAT
Feed your dragons daily.	○	○	○	○	○	○	○
Change water daily.	○	○	○	○	○	○	○
Dusting powder on food 1 x / 2-3 day.	○	○	○	○	○	○	○
Remove any uneaten live food	○	○	○	○	○	○	○
Spot clean soiled areas	○	○	○	○	○	○	○
Check temperatures / humidity	○	○	○	○	○	○	○
Visually inspect Bearded Dragon	○	○	○	○	○	○	○

NOTES:

BEARDED DRAGON CHECKLIST

📅 DATE:

📅 DATE:

WEEKLY ACTIVITY

Clean glass

Top up substrate

Clean any decorative rocks, plants etc

Physically inspect your dragon

Bathing dragon &
trim toenails once a week

Weigh & record data

HEALTH CHECKLIST

Active and alert

Clear eyes

Body and tail are
filled out

Healthy skin

Clear nose and vent

Eats regularly

DIARY / NOTES:

BEARDED DRAGON CHECKLIST

 Daily Activity

WEEK OF [ ] DATE [ ]

	SUN	MON	TUE	WED	THU	FRI	SAT
Feed your dragons daily.	○	○	○	○	○	○	○
Change water daily.	○	○	○	○	○	○	○
Dusting powder on food 1 x / 2-3 day.	○	○	○	○	○	○	○
Remove any uneaten live food	○	○	○	○	○	○	○
Spot clean soiled areas	○	○	○	○	○	○	○
Check temperatures / humidity	○	○	○	○	○	○	○
Visually inspect Bearded Dragon	○	○	○	○	○	○	○

NOTES:

BEARDED DRAGON CHECKLIST

📅 DATE: _____   📅 DATE: _____

WEEKLY ACTIVITY

○ Clean glass

○ Top up substrate

○ Clean any decorative rocks, plants etc

○ Physically inspect your dragon

○ Bathing dragon &
trim toenails once a week

○ Weigh & record data

HEALTH CHECKLIST

○ Active and alert

○ Clear eyes

○ Body and tail are
filled out

○ Healthy skin

○ Clear nose and vent

○ Eats regularly

DIARY / NOTES:

BEARDED DRAGON CHECKLIST

 Daily Activity

WEEK OF [ ] DATE [ ]

	SUN	MON	TUE	WED	THU	FRI	SAT
Feed your dragons daily.	○	○	○	○	○	○	○
Change water daily.	○	○	○	○	○	○	○
Dusting powder on food 1 x / 2-3 day.	○	○	○	○	○	○	○
Remove any uneaten live food	○	○	○	○	○	○	○
Spot clean soiled areas	○	○	○	○	○	○	○
Check temperatures / humidity	○	○	○	○	○	○	○
Visually inspect Bearded Dragon	○	○	○	○	○	○	○

NOTES:

BEARDED DRAGON CHECKLIST

📅 DATE:

📅 DATE:

WEEKLY ACTIVITY

- Clean glass

- Top up substrate

- Clean any decorative rocks, plants etc

- Physically inspect your dragon

- Bathing dragon &
trim toenails once a week

- Weigh & record data

HEALTH CHECKLIST

- Active and alert

- Clear eyes

- Body and tail are
filled out

- Healthy skin

- Clear nose and vent

- Eats regularly

DIARY / NOTES:

BEARDED DRAGON CHECKLIST

Daily Activity	WEEK OF [ ] DATE [ ]						
	SUN	MON	TUE	WED	THU	FRI	SAT
Feed your dragons daily.	○	○	○	○	○	○	○
Change water daily.	○	○	○	○	○	○	○
Dusting powder on food 1 x / 2-3 day.	○	○	○	○	○	○	○
Remove any uneaten live food	○	○	○	○	○	○	○
Spot clean soiled areas	○	○	○	○	○	○	○
Check temperatures / humidity	○	○	○	○	○	○	○
Visually inspect Bearded Dragon	○	○	○	○	○	○	○

NOTES:

BEARDED DRAGON CHECKLIST

📅 DATE: _____   📅 DATE: _____

WEEKLY ACTIVITY

- ○ Clean glass
- ○ Top up substrate
- ○ Clean any decorative rocks, plants etc
- ○ Physically inspect your dragon
- ○ Bathing dragon & trim toenails once a week
- ○ Weigh & record data

HEALTH CHECKLIST

- ○ Active and alert
- ○ Clear eyes
- ○ Body and tail are filled out
- ○ Healthy skin
- ○ Clear nose and vent
- ○ Eats regularly

DIARY / NOTES:

BEARDED DRAGON CHECKLIST

 Daily Activity

WEEK OF _____ DATE _____

	SUN	MON	TUE	WED	THU	FRI	SAT
Feed your dragons daily.	◯	◯	◯	◯	◯	◯	◯
Change water daily.	◯	◯	◯	◯	◯	◯	◯
Dusting powder on food 1 x / 2-3 day.	◯	◯	◯	◯	◯	◯	◯
Remove any uneaten live food	◯	◯	◯	◯	◯	◯	◯
Spot clean soiled areas	◯	◯	◯	◯	◯	◯	◯
Check temperatures / humidity	◯	◯	◯	◯	◯	◯	◯
Visually inspect Bearded Dragon	◯	◯	◯	◯	◯	◯	◯

NOTES:

BEARDED DRAGON CHECKLIST

📅 DATE: _____

📅 DATE: _____

WEEKLY ACTIVITY

○ Clean glass

○ Top up substrate

○ Clean any decorative rocks, plants etc

○ Physically inspect your dragon

○ Bathing dragon &
trim toenails once a week

○ Weigh & record data

HEALTH CHECKLIST

○ Active and alert

○ Clear eyes

○ Body and tail are
filled out

○ Healthy skin

○ Clear nose and vent

○ Eats regularly

DIARY / NOTES:

BEARDED DRAGON CHECKLIST

Daily Activity	WEEK OF [ ] DATE [ ]						
	SUN	MON	TUE	WED	THU	FRI	SAT
Feed your dragons daily.	○	○	○	○	○	○	○
Change water daily.	○	○	○	○	○	○	○
Dusting powder on food 1 x / 2-3 day.	○	○	○	○	○	○	○
Remove any uneaten live food	○	○	○	○	○	○	○
Spot clean soiled areas	○	○	○	○	○	○	○
Check temperatures / humidity	○	○	○	○	○	○	○
Visually inspect Bearded Dragon	○	○	○	○	○	○	○

NOTES:

BEARDED DRAGON CHECKLIST

📅 DATE: _____   📅 DATE: _____

WEEKLY ACTIVITY

- ○ Clean glass
- ○ Top up substrate
- ○ Clean any decorative rocks, plants etc
- ○ Physically inspect your dragon
- ○ Bathing dragon & trim toenails once a week
- ○ Weigh & record data

HEALTH CHECKLIST

- ○ Active and alert
- ○ Clear eyes
- ○ Body and tail are filled out
- ○ Healthy skin
- ○ Clear nose and vent
- ○ Eats regularly

DIARY / NOTES:

BEARDED DRAGON CHECKLIST

 Daily Activity

WEEK OF _____ DATE _____

	SUN	MON	TUE	WED	THU	FRI	SAT
Feed your dragons daily.	○	○	○	○	○	○	○
Change water daily.	○	○	○	○	○	○	○
Dusting powder on food 1 x / 2-3 day.	○	○	○	○	○	○	○
Remove any uneaten live food	○	○	○	○	○	○	○
Spot clean soiled areas	○	○	○	○	○	○	○
Check temperatures / humidity	○	○	○	○	○	○	○
Visually inspect Bearded Dragon	○	○	○	○	○	○	○

NOTES:

BEARDED DRAGON CHECKLIST

📅 DATE:

📅 DATE:

WEEKLY ACTIVITY

Clean glass

Top up substrate

Clean any decorative rocks, plants etc

Physically inspect your dragon

Bathing dragon &
trim toenails once a week

Weigh & record data

HEALTH CHECKLIST

Active and alert

Clear eyes

Body and tail are
filled out

Healthy skin

Clear nose and vent

Eats regularly

DIARY / NOTES:

BEARDED DRAGON CHECKLIST

 Daily Activity

WEEK OF		DATE				
SUN	MON	TUE	WED	THU	FRI	SAT

 Feed your dragons daily.

| ○ | ○ | ○ | ○ | ○ | ○ | ○ |

 Change water daily.

| ○ | ○ | ○ | ○ | ○ | ○ | ○ |

 Dusting powder on food 1 x / 2-3 day.

| ○ | ○ | ○ | ○ | ○ | ○ | ○ |

 Remove any uneaten live food

| ○ | ○ | ○ | ○ | ○ | ○ | ○ |

 Spot clean soiled areas

| ○ | ○ | ○ | ○ | ○ | ○ | ○ |

 Check temperatures / humidity

| ○ | ○ | ○ | ○ | ○ | ○ | ○ |

 Visually inspect Bearded Dragon

| ○ | ○ | ○ | ○ | ○ | ○ | ○ |

NOTES:

BEARDED DRAGON CHECKLIST

📅 DATE: [   ]   📅 DATE: [   ]

WEEKLY ACTIVITY

- ○ Clean glass
- ○ Top up substrate
- ○ Clean any decorative rocks, plants etc
- ○ Physically inspect your dragon
- ○ Bathing dragon & trim toenails once a week
- ○ Weigh & record data

HEALTH CHECKLIST

- ○ Active and alert
- ○ Clear eyes
- ○ Body and tail are filled out
- ○ Healthy skin
- ○ Clear nose and vent
- ○ Eats regularly

DIARY / NOTES:

BEARDED DRAGON CHECKLIST

 Daily Activity

WEEK OF [ ]   DATE [ ]

	SUN	MON	TUE	WED	THU	FRI	SAT
Feed your dragons daily.	◯	◯	◯	◯	◯	◯	◯
Change water daily.	◯	◯	◯	◯	◯	◯	◯
Dusting powder on food 1 x / 2-3 day.	◯	◯	◯	◯	◯	◯	◯
Remove any uneaten live food	◯	◯	◯	◯	◯	◯	◯
Spot clean soiled areas	◯	◯	◯	◯	◯	◯	◯
Check temperatures / humidity	◯	◯	◯	◯	◯	◯	◯
Visually inspect Bearded Dragon	◯	◯	◯	◯	◯	◯	◯

NOTES:

BEARDED DRAGON CHECKLIST

📅 DATE: _____

📅 DATE: _____

WEEKLY ACTIVITY

Clean glass

Top up substrate

Clean any decorative rocks, plants etc

Physically inspect your dragon

Bathing dragon &
trim toenails once a week

Weigh & record data

HEALTH CHECKLIST

Active and alert

Clear eyes

Body and tail are
filled out

Healthy skin

Clear nose and vent

Eats regularly

DIARY / NOTES:

BEARDED DRAGON CHECKLIST

	Daily Activity	WEEK OF DATE						
		SUN	MON	TUE	WED	THU	FRI	SAT
	Feed your dragons daily.	○	○	○	○	○	○	○
	Change water daily.	○	○	○	○	○	○	○
	Dusting powder on food 1 x / 2-3 day.	○	○	○	○	○	○	○
	Remove any uneaten live food	○	○	○	○	○	○	○
	Spot clean soiled areas	○	○	○	○	○	○	○
	Check temperatures / humidity	○	○	○	○	○	○	○
	Visually inspect Bearded Dragon	○	○	○	○	○	○	○

NOTES:

BEARDED DRAGON CHECKLIST

📅 DATE: _____   📅 DATE: _____

WEEKLY ACTIVITY

○ Clean glass

○ Top up substrate

○ Clean any decorative rocks, plants etc

○ Physically inspect your dragon

○ Bathing dragon &
trim toenails once a week

○ Weigh & record data

HEALTH CHECKLIST

○ Active and alert

○ Clear eyes

○ Body and tail are
filled out

○ Healthy skin

○ Clear nose and vent

○ Eats regularly

DIARY / NOTES:

BEARDED DRAGON CHECKLIST

 Daily Activity

WEEK OF [   ] DATE [   ]

	SUN	MON	TUE	WED	THU	FRI	SAT
Feed your dragons daily.	○	○	○	○	○	○	○
Change water daily.	○	○	○	○	○	○	○
Dusting powder on food 1 x / 2-3 day.	○	○	○	○	○	○	○
Remove any uneaten live food	○	○	○	○	○	○	○
Spot clean soiled areas	○	○	○	○	○	○	○
Check temperatures / humidity	○	○	○	○	○	○	○
Visually inspect Bearded Dragon	○	○	○	○	○	○	○

NOTES:

BEARDED DRAGON CHECKLIST

📅 DATE: _____   📅 DATE: _____

WEEKLY ACTIVITY

Clean glass

Top up substrate

Clean any decorative rocks, plants etc

Physically inspect your dragon

Bathing dragon &
trim toenails once a week

Weigh & record data

HEALTH CHECKLIST

Active and alert

Clear eyes

Body and tail are
filled out

Healthy skin

Clear nose and vent

Eats regularly

DIARY / NOTES:

BEARDED DRAGON CHECKLIST

 Daily Activity

WEEK OF [ ] DATE [ ]

	SUN	MON	TUE	WED	THU	FRI	SAT
Feed your dragons daily.	○	○	○	○	○	○	○
Change water daily.	○	○	○	○	○	○	○
Dusting powder on food 1 x / 2-3 day.	○	○	○	○	○	○	○
Remove any uneaten live food	○	○	○	○	○	○	○
Spot clean soiled areas	○	○	○	○	○	○	○
Check temperatures / humidity	○	○	○	○	○	○	○
Visually inspect Bearded Dragon	○	○	○	○	○	○	○

NOTES:

BEARDED DRAGON CHECKLIST

📅 DATE: _____   📅 DATE: _____

WEEKLY ACTIVITY

- ⬤ Clean glass
- ⬤ Top up substrate
- ⬤ Clean any decorative rocks, plants etc
- ⬤ Physically inspect your dragon
- ⬤ Bathing dragon & trim toenails once a week
- ⬤ Weigh & record data

HEALTH CHECKLIST

- ⬤ Active and alert
- ⬤ Clear eyes
- ⬤ Body and tail are filled out
- ⬤ Healthy skin
- ⬤ Clear nose and vent
- ⬤ Eats regularly

DIARY / NOTES:

BEARDED DRAGON CHECKLIST

 Daily Activity

	SUN	MON	TUE	WED	THU	FRI	SAT

WEEK OF [ ]   DATE [ ]

 Feed your dragons daily.
○ ○ ○ ○ ○ ○ ○

 Change water daily.
○ ○ ○ ○ ○ ○ ○

 Dusting powder on food 1 x / 2-3 day.
○ ○ ○ ○ ○ ○ ○

 Remove any uneaten live food
○ ○ ○ ○ ○ ○ ○

 Spot clean soiled areas
○ ○ ○ ○ ○ ○ ○

 Check temperatures / humidity
○ ○ ○ ○ ○ ○ ○

 Visually inspect Bearded Dragon
○ ○ ○ ○ ○ ○ ○

NOTES:

BEARDED DRAGON CHECKLIST

📅 DATE:

📅 DATE:

WEEKLY ACTIVITY

Clean glass

Top up substrate

Clean any decorative rocks, plants etc

Physically inspect your dragon

Bathing dragon &
trim toenails once a week

Weigh & record data

HEALTH CHECKLIST

Active and alert

Clear eyes

Body and tail are
filled out

Healthy skin

Clear nose and vent

Eats regularly

DIARY / NOTES:

BEARDED DRAGON CHECKLIST

 Daily Activity

WEEK OF [ ] DATE [ ]

	SUN	MON	TUE	WED	THU	FRI	SAT
Feed your dragons daily.	○	○	○	○	○	○	○
Change water daily.	○	○	○	○	○	○	○
Dusting powder on food 1 x / 2-3 day.	○	○	○	○	○	○	○
Remove any uneaten live food	○	○	○	○	○	○	○
Spot clean soiled areas	○	○	○	○	○	○	○
Check temperatures / humidity	○	○	○	○	○	○	○
Visually inspect Bearded Dragon	○	○	○	○	○	○	○

NOTES:

BEARDED DRAGON CHECKLIST

📅 DATE: _____

📅 DATE: _____

WEEKLY ACTIVITY

○ Clean glass

○ Top up substrate

○ Clean any decorative rocks, plants etc

○ Physically inspect your dragon

○ Bathing dragon &
trim toenails once a week

○ Weigh & record data

HEALTH CHECKLIST

○ Active and alert

○ Clear eyes

○ Body and tail are
filled out

○ Healthy skin

○ Clear nose and vent

○ Eats regularly

DIARY / NOTES:

BEARDED DRAGON CHECKLIST

 Daily Activity

WEEK OF ☐ DATE ☐

Activity	SUN	MON	TUE	WED	THU	FRI	SAT
Feed your dragons daily.	○	○	○	○	○	○	○
Change water daily.	○	○	○	○	○	○	○
Dusting powder on food 1 x / 2-3 day.	○	○	○	○	○	○	○
Remove any uneaten live food	○	○	○	○	○	○	○
Spot clean soiled areas	○	○	○	○	○	○	○
Check temperatures / humidity	○	○	○	○	○	○	○
Visually inspect Bearded Dragon	○	○	○	○	○	○	○

NOTES:

BEARDED DRAGON CHECKLIST

📅 DATE: _____   📅 DATE: _____

WEEKLY ACTIVITY

○ Clean glass

○ Top up substrate

○ Clean any decorative rocks, plants etc

○ Physically inspect your dragon

○ Bathing dragon &
trim toenails once a week

○ Weigh & record data

HEALTH CHECKLIST

○ Active and alert

○ Clear eyes

○ Body and tail are
filled out

○ Healthy skin

○ Clear nose and vent

○ Eats regularly

DIARY / NOTES:

BEARDED DRAGON CHECKLIST

 Daily Activity

WEEK OF [   ]   DATE [   ]

	SUN	MON	TUE	WED	THU	FRI	SAT
Feed your dragons daily.	◯	◯	◯	◯	◯	◯	◯
Change water daily.	◯	◯	◯	◯	◯	◯	◯
Dusting powder on food 1 x / 2-3 day.	◯	◯	◯	◯	◯	◯	◯
Remove any uneaten live food	◯	◯	◯	◯	◯	◯	◯
Spot clean soiled areas	◯	◯	◯	◯	◯	◯	◯
Check temperatures / humidity	◯	◯	◯	◯	◯	◯	◯
Visually inspect Bearded Dragon	◯	◯	◯	◯	◯	◯	◯

NOTES:

BEARDED DRAGON CHECKLIST

📅 DATE: [   ]   📅 DATE: [   ]

WEEKLY ACTIVITY

- ○ Clean glass
- ○ Top up substrate
- ○ Clean any decorative rocks, plants etc
- ○ Physically inspect your dragon
- ○ Bathing dragon & trim toenails once a week
- ○ Weigh & record data

HEALTH CHECKLIST

- ○ Active and alert
- ○ Clear eyes
- ○ Body and tail are filled out
- ○ Healthy skin
- ○ Clear nose and vent
- ○ Eats regularly

DIARY / NOTES:

BEARDED DRAGON CHECKLIST

 Daily Activity

WEEK OF [   ] DATE [   ]

	SUN	MON	TUE	WED	THU	FRI	SAT
Feed your dragons daily.	○	○	○	○	○	○	○
Change water daily.	○	○	○	○	○	○	○
Dusting powder on food 1 x / 2-3 day.	○	○	○	○	○	○	○
Remove any uneaten live food	○	○	○	○	○	○	○
Spot clean soiled areas	○	○	○	○	○	○	○
Check temperatures / humidity	○	○	○	○	○	○	○
Visually inspect Bearded Dragon	○	○	○	○	○	○	○

NOTES:

BEARDED DRAGON CHECKLIST

📅 DATE:

📅 DATE:

WEEKLY ACTIVITY

Clean glass

Top up substrate

Clean any decorative rocks, plants etc

Physically inspect your dragon

Bathing dragon &
trim toenails once a week

Weigh & record data

HEALTH CHECKLIST

Active and alert

Clear eyes

Body and tail are
filled out

Healthy skin

Clear nose and vent

Eats regularly

DIARY / NOTES:

BEARDED DRAGON CHECKLIST

 Daily Activity

WEEK OF [ ] DATE [ ]

	SUN	MON	TUE	WED	THU	FRI	SAT
Feed your dragons daily.	○	○	○	○	○	○	○
Change water daily.	○	○	○	○	○	○	○
Dusting powder on food 1 x / 2-3 day.	○	○	○	○	○	○	○
Remove any uneaten live food	○	○	○	○	○	○	○
Spot clean soiled areas	○	○	○	○	○	○	○
Check temperatures / humidity	○	○	○	○	○	○	○
Visually inspect Bearded Dragon	○	○	○	○	○	○	○

NOTES:

BEARDED DRAGON CHECKLIST

📅 DATE: _____   📅 DATE: _____

WEEKLY ACTIVITY

- ◯ Clean glass
- ◯ Top up substrate
- ◯ Clean any decorative rocks, plants etc
- ◯ Physically inspect your dragon
- ◯ Bathing dragon & trim toenails once a week
- ◯ Weigh & record data

HEALTH CHECKLIST

- ◯ Active and alert
- ◯ Clear eyes
- ◯ Body and tail are filled out
- ◯ Healthy skin
- ◯ Clear nose and vent
- ◯ Eats regularly

DIARY / NOTES:

BEARDED DRAGON CHECKLIST

 Daily Activity

WEEK OF [   ] DATE [   ]

	SUN	MON	TUE	WED	THU	FRI	SAT

 Feed your dragons daily.

SUN	MON	TUE	WED	THU	FRI	SAT
○	○	○	○	○	○	○

 Change water daily.

SUN	MON	TUE	WED	THU	FRI	SAT
○	○	○	○	○	○	○

 Dusting powder on food 1 x / 2-3 day.

SUN	MON	TUE	WED	THU	FRI	SAT
○	○	○	○	○	○	○

 Remove any uneaten live food

SUN	MON	TUE	WED	THU	FRI	SAT
○	○	○	○	○	○	○

 Spot clean soiled areas

SUN	MON	TUE	WED	THU	FRI	SAT
○	○	○	○	○	○	○

 Check temperatures / humidity

SUN	MON	TUE	WED	THU	FRI	SAT
○	○	○	○	○	○	○

 Visually inspect Bearded Dragon

SUN	MON	TUE	WED	THU	FRI	SAT
○	○	○	○	○	○	○

NOTES:

BEARDED DRAGON CHECKLIST

📅 DATE: _____   📅 DATE: _____

WEEKLY ACTIVITY

- Clean glass
- Top up substrate
- Clean any decorative rocks, plants etc
- Physically inspect your dragon
- Bathing dragon & trim toenails once a week
- Weigh & record data

HEALTH CHECKLIST

- Active and alert
- Clear eyes
- Body and tail are filled out
- Healthy skin
- Clear nose and vent
- Eats regularly

DIARY / NOTES:

BEARDED DRAGON CHECKLIST

 Daily Activity

WEEK OF		DATE				
SUN	MON	TUE	WED	THU	FRI	SAT

 Feed your dragons daily. ○ ○ ○ ○ ○ ○ ○

 Change water daily. ○ ○ ○ ○ ○ ○ ○

 Dusting powder on food 1 x / 2-3 day. ○ ○ ○ ○ ○ ○ ○

 Remove any uneaten live food ○ ○ ○ ○ ○ ○ ○

 Spot clean soiled areas ○ ○ ○ ○ ○ ○ ○

 Check temperatures / humidity ○ ○ ○ ○ ○ ○ ○

 Visually inspect Bearded Dragon ○ ○ ○ ○ ○ ○ ○

NOTES:

BEARDED DRAGON CHECKLIST

📅 DATE: [_____]

📅 DATE: [_____]

WEEKLY ACTIVITY

○ Clean glass

○ Top up substrate

○ Clean any decorative rocks, plants etc

○ Physically inspect your dragon

○ Bathing dragon &
trim toenails once a week

○ Weigh & record data

HEALTH CHECKLIST

○ Active and alert

○ Clear eyes

○ Body and tail are
filled out

○ Healthy skin

○ Clear nose and vent

○ Eats regularly

DIARY / NOTES:

BEARDED DRAGON CHECKLIST

 Daily Activity

WEEK OF [   ] DATE [   ]

	SUN	MON	TUE	WED	THU	FRI	SAT
Feed your dragons daily.	○	○	○	○	○	○	○
Change water daily.	○	○	○	○	○	○	○
Dusting powder on food 1 x / 2-3 day.	○	○	○	○	○	○	○
Remove any uneaten live food	○	○	○	○	○	○	○
Spot clean soiled areas	○	○	○	○	○	○	○
Check temperatures / humidity	○	○	○	○	○	○	○
Visually inspect Bearded Dragon	○	○	○	○	○	○	○

NOTES:

BEARDED DRAGON CHECKLIST

📅 DATE: _____   📅 DATE: _____

WEEKLY ACTIVITY

○ Clean glass

○ Top up substrate

○ Clean any decorative rocks, plants etc

○ Physically inspect your dragon

○ Bathing dragon &
  trim toenails once a week

○ Weigh & record data

HEALTH CHECKLIST

○ Active and alert

○ Clear eyes

○ Body and tail are
  filled out

○ Healthy skin

○ Clear nose and vent

○ Eats regularly

DIARY / NOTES:

BEARDED DRAGON CHECKLIST

 Daily Activity

WEEK OF [   ] DATE [   ]

	SUN	MON	TUE	WED	THU	FRI	SAT
Feed your dragons daily.	○	○	○	○	○	○	○
Change water daily.	○	○	○	○	○	○	○
Dusting powder on food 1 x / 2-3 day.	○	○	○	○	○	○	○
Remove any uneaten live food	○	○	○	○	○	○	○
Spot clean soiled areas	○	○	○	○	○	○	○
Check temperatures / humidity	○	○	○	○	○	○	○
Visually inspect Bearded Dragon	○	○	○	○	○	○	○

NOTES:

BEARDED DRAGON CHECKLIST

📅 DATE: _____　　　　📅 DATE: _____

WEEKLY ACTIVITY

○ Clean glass

○ Top up substrate

○ Clean any decorative rocks, plants etc

○ Physically inspect your dragon

○ Bathing dragon &
  trim toenails once a week

○ Weigh & record data

HEALTH CHECKLIST

○ Active and alert

○ Clear eyes

○ Body and tail are
  filled out

○ Healthy skin

○ Clear nose and vent

○ Eats regularly

DIARY / NOTES:

BEARDED DRAGON CHECKLIST

 Daily Activity

WEEK OF _____ DATE _____

	SUN	MON	TUE	WED	THU	FRI	SAT
Feed your dragons daily.	○	○	○	○	○	○	○
Change water daily.	○	○	○	○	○	○	○
Dusting powder on food 1 x / 2-3 day.	○	○	○	○	○	○	○
Remove any uneaten live food	○	○	○	○	○	○	○
Spot clean soiled areas	○	○	○	○	○	○	○
Check temperatures / humidity	○	○	○	○	○	○	○
Visually inspect Bearded Dragon	○	○	○	○	○	○	○

NOTES:

BEARDED DRAGON CHECKLIST

📅 DATE: _____   📅 DATE: _____

WEEKLY ACTIVITY

Clean glass

Top up substrate

Clean any decorative rocks, plants etc

Physically inspect your dragon

Bathing dragon &
trim toenails once a week

Weigh & record data

HEALTH CHECKLIST

Active and alert

Clear eyes

Body and tail are
filled out

Healthy skin

Clear nose and vent

Eats regularly

DIARY / NOTES:

BEARDED DRAGON CHECKLIST

 Daily Activity

	WEEK OF ___ DATE ___						
	SUN	MON	TUE	WED	THU	FRI	SAT
Feed your dragons daily.	○	○	○	○	○	○	○
Change water daily.	○	○	○	○	○	○	○
Dusting powder on food 1 x / 2-3 day.	○	○	○	○	○	○	○
Remove any uneaten live food	○	○	○	○	○	○	○
Spot clean soiled areas	○	○	○	○	○	○	○
Check temperatures / humidity	○	○	○	○	○	○	○
Visually inspect Bearded Dragon	○	○	○	○	○	○	○

NOTES:

BEARDED DRAGON CHECKLIST

📅 DATE: _____   📅 DATE: _____

WEEKLY ACTIVITY

○ Clean glass

○ Top up substrate

○ Clean any decorative rocks, plants etc

○ Physically inspect your dragon

○ Bathing dragon &
trim toenails once a week

○ Weigh & record data

HEALTH CHECKLIST

○ Active and alert

○ Clear eyes

○ Body and tail are
filled out

○ Healthy skin

○ Clear nose and vent

○ Eats regularly

DIARY / NOTES:

BEARDED DRAGON CHECKLIST

 Daily Activity

WEEK OF [   ] DATE [   ]

	SUN	MON	TUE	WED	THU	FRI	SAT
Feed your dragons daily.	○	○	○	○	○	○	○
Change water daily.	○	○	○	○	○	○	○
Dusting powder on food 1 x / 2-3 day.	○	○	○	○	○	○	○
Remove any uneaten live food	○	○	○	○	○	○	○
Spot clean soiled areas	○	○	○	○	○	○	○
Check temperatures / humidity	○	○	○	○	○	○	○
Visually inspect Bearded Dragon	○	○	○	○	○	○	○

NOTES:

BEARDED DRAGON CHECKLIST

📅 DATE:

📅 DATE:

WEEKLY ACTIVITY

Clean glass

Top up substrate

Clean any decorative rocks, plants etc

Physically inspect your dragon

Bathing dragon &
trim toenails once a week

Weigh & record data

HEALTH CHECKLIST

Active and alert

Clear eyes

Body and tail are
filled out

Healthy skin

Clear nose and vent

Eats regularly

DIARY / NOTES:

BEARDED DRAGON CHECKLIST

 Daily Activity

	WEEK OF	DATE					
	SUN	MON	TUE	WED	THU	FRI	SAT
Feed your dragons daily.	○	○	○	○	○	○	○
Change water daily.	○	○	○	○	○	○	○
Dusting powder on food 1 x / 2-3 day.	○	○	○	○	○	○	○
Remove any uneaten live food	○	○	○	○	○	○	○
Spot clean soiled areas	○	○	○	○	○	○	○
Check temperatures / humidity	○	○	○	○	○	○	○
Visually inspect Bearded Dragon	○	○	○	○	○	○	○

NOTES:

BEARDED DRAGON CHECKLIST

📅 DATE: _____   📅 DATE: _____

WEEKLY ACTIVITY

○ Clean glass

○ Top up substrate

○ Clean any decorative rocks, plants etc

○ Physically inspect your dragon

○ Bathing dragon &
trim toenails once a week

○ Weigh & record data

HEALTH CHECKLIST

○ Active and alert

○ Clear eyes

○ Body and tail are
filled out

○ Healthy skin

○ Clear nose and vent

○ Eats regularly

DIARY / NOTES:

BEARDED DRAGON CHECKLIST

 Daily Activity

	WEEK OF		DATE			
SUN	MON	TUE	WED	THU	FRI	SAT

 Feed your dragons daily.

| ○ | ○ | ○ | ○ | ○ | ○ | ○ |

 Change water daily.

| ○ | ○ | ○ | ○ | ○ | ○ | ○ |

 Dusting powder on food 1 x / 2-3 day.

| ○ | ○ | ○ | ○ | ○ | ○ | ○ |

 Remove any uneaten live food

| ○ | ○ | ○ | ○ | ○ | ○ | ○ |

 Spot clean soiled areas

| ○ | ○ | ○ | ○ | ○ | ○ | ○ |

 Check temperatures / humidity

| ○ | ○ | ○ | ○ | ○ | ○ | ○ |

 Visually inspect Bearded Dragon

| ○ | ○ | ○ | ○ | ○ | ○ | ○ |

NOTES:

BEARDED DRAGON CHECKLIST

📅 DATE: _____   📅 DATE: _____

WEEKLY ACTIVITY

Clean glass

Top up substrate

Clean any decorative rocks, plants etc

Physically inspect your dragon

Bathing dragon &
trim toenails once a week

Weigh & record data

HEALTH CHECKLIST

Active and alert

Clear eyes

Body and tail are
filled out

Healthy skin

Clear nose and vent

Eats regularly

DIARY / NOTES:

BEARDED DRAGON CHECKLIST

 Daily Activity

WEEK OF [ ] DATE [ ]

	SUN	MON	TUE	WED	THU	FRI	SAT
Feed your dragons daily.	○	○	○	○	○	○	○
Change water daily.	○	○	○	○	○	○	○
Dusting powder on food 1 x / 2-3 day.	○	○	○	○	○	○	○
Remove any uneaten live food	○	○	○	○	○	○	○
Spot clean soiled areas	○	○	○	○	○	○	○
Check temperatures / humidity	○	○	○	○	○	○	○
Visually inspect Bearded Dragon	○	○	○	○	○	○	○

NOTES:

BEARDED DRAGON CHECKLIST

📅 DATE: _____   📅 DATE: _____

WEEKLY ACTIVITY

- ○ Clean glass
- ○ Top up substrate
- ○ Clean any decorative rocks, plants etc
- ○ Physically inspect your dragon
- ○ Bathing dragon & trim toenails once a week
- ○ Weigh & record data

HEALTH CHECKLIST

- ○ Active and alert
- ○ Clear eyes
- ○ Body and tail are filled out
- ○ Healthy skin
- ○ Clear nose and vent
- ○ Eats regularly

DIARY / NOTES:

BEARDED DRAGON CHECKLIST

 Daily Activity

	WEEK OF DATE						
	SUN	MON	TUE	WED	THU	FRI	SAT
Feed your dragons daily.	○	○	○	○	○	○	○
Change water daily.	○	○	○	○	○	○	○
Dusting powder on food 1 x / 2-3 day.	○	○	○	○	○	○	○
Remove any uneaten live food	○	○	○	○	○	○	○
Spot clean soiled areas	○	○	○	○	○	○	○
Check temperatures / humidity	○	○	○	○	○	○	○
Visually inspect Bearded Dragon	○	○	○	○	○	○	○

NOTES:

BEARDED DRAGON CHECKLIST

📅 DATE:

📅 DATE:

WEEKLY ACTIVITY

Clean glass

Top up substrate

Clean any decorative rocks, plants etc

Physically inspect your dragon

Bathing dragon &
trim toenails once a week

Weigh & record data

HEALTH CHECKLIST

Active and alert

Clear eyes

Body and tail are
filled out

Healthy skin

Clear nose and vent

Eats regularly

DIARY / NOTES:

BEARDED DRAGON CHECKLIST

 Daily Activity

WEEK OF [   ] DATE [   ]

	SUN	MON	TUE	WED	THU	FRI	SAT
Feed your dragons daily.	○	○	○	○	○	○	○
Change water daily.	○	○	○	○	○	○	○
Dusting powder on food 1 x / 2-3 day.	○	○	○	○	○	○	○
Remove any uneaten live food	○	○	○	○	○	○	○
Spot clean soiled areas	○	○	○	○	○	○	○
Check temperatures / humidity	○	○	○	○	○	○	○
Visually inspect Bearded Dragon	○	○	○	○	○	○	○

NOTES:

BEARDED DRAGON CHECKLIST

📅 DATE: _____

📅 DATE: _____

WEEKLY ACTIVITY

- ○ Clean glass
- ○ Top up substrate
- ○ Clean any decorative rocks, plants etc
- ○ Physically inspect your dragon
- ○ Bathing dragon & trim toenails once a week
- ○ Weigh & record data

HEALTH CHECKLIST

- ○ Active and alert
- ○ Clear eyes
- ○ Body and tail are filled out
- ○ Healthy skin
- ○ Clear nose and vent
- ○ Eats regularly

DIARY / NOTES:

BEARDED DRAGON CHECKLIST

 Daily Activity

WEEK OF	DATE					
SUN	MON	TUE	WED	THU	FRI	SAT

 Feed your dragons daily.

○ ○ ○ ○ ○ ○ ○

 Change water daily.

○ ○ ○ ○ ○ ○ ○

 Dusting powder on food 1 x / 2-3 day.

○ ○ ○ ○ ○ ○ ○

 Remove any uneaten live food

○ ○ ○ ○ ○ ○ ○

 Spot clean soiled areas

○ ○ ○ ○ ○ ○ ○

 Check temperatures / humidity

○ ○ ○ ○ ○ ○ ○

 Visually inspect Bearded Dragon

○ ○ ○ ○ ○ ○ ○

NOTES:

BEARDED DRAGON CHECKLIST

📅 DATE: _____

📅 DATE: _____

WEEKLY ACTIVITY

Clean glass

Top up substrate

Clean any decorative rocks, plants etc

Physically inspect your dragon

Bathing dragon &
trim toenails once a week

Weigh & record data

HEALTH CHECKLIST

Active and alert

Clear eyes

Body and tail are
filled out

Healthy skin

Clear nose and vent

Eats regularly

DIARY / NOTES:

Made in United States
Orlando, FL
21 September 2024

51791317R00070